To Daughter a Devil

MEGAN MARY MOORE

For the woman who daughtered her own devil, my mom.

This is the way of an adulterous woman: she eats and wipes her mouth and says, 'I've done nothing wrong.'

— Proverbs 30:20

Poems

To Daughter a Devil

MEGAN MARY MOORE

The Hickory Horned Devil

has orange horns protruding from her green body
because she has seen beaks and teeth
sink into new, fleshy skin too many times
and she will not be touched.
Spikes so fierce even chickens run,
But when asked, entomologists hiss
Harmless.

II

In gym class she picks at the grass
and lets the Devil crawl over her hands.
16 legs tickling her cuticles
and she remembers feeling
her fontanelle harden.
Bone reaching for bone,
an ache she'd grow to know
just by looking at her mother.

An ache that mostly feels like
the absence of
elbow scrapes,

dirty fingernails,
poolwater in her nose.

She brings the Devil to her face,
inviting her to her cheek
The class stops kicking the ball,
watches the Devil creep
over her lips. The gym teacher sighs
Someday you will outgrow this.

III

The Devil fights histolysis
with all of her horns
because somewhere in her body,
tucked behind her guts,
is the understanding that,
after staving off beak and teeth,
when she emerges,
soft and big,
the regal moth lives
for one week. She flies
as hard as she can
to mate and make
babies until she dies
of exhaustion.

Evil Lives in Sweet In Between Spaces

What I mean is,   what if
Regan was never possessed?

What if she wet herself at the dinner party,
she spewed green and asked,
Do you know what she did?
Your cunting daughter?
And the answer was
everything.

What if Father Karras killed himself
before accepting that
—without demonic force—
Regan could be, would be
so   ugly?

Baby Bezoar

 A fourteen-pound hairball
was removed from her stomach.
A bezoar she'd been feeding
with every strand she sucked.

Do you think she got to keep it?

Did she let it rent space in her body,
then say sayonara
to her intestines' tenant
in a biomedical waste bag?

Do you think it was like a baby?

A being removed from womb,
to roll on, collect hair elsewhere,
until it finds somewhere to lay down
and reminisce about its mother
to whom it only caused pain.

After Rosemary Picked Up the Baby

She chose to bottle feed because of his full set of adult teeth.
It's breast milk. I pump, she assured anyone in earshot.

She used the "cry it out" method to get him to sleep.
Research shows it's better for mom and baby, she insisted,
   red-eyed.

She didn't use a sleep sack or swaddle.
He loves to thrash! she laughed.

His first word was daddy.
She didn't have anything to say about that.

Mrs. Vorhees to the Camp Counselor

I'm doing what mothers do.
You would have understood
if you had lived long enough
to forget your own name
and only remember whose
mother you are.

For every girl in a string bikini
there is a mother who remembers
the freedom to look away from noise
toward sun, her eyes
asking to be touched. And how that touch
drowns the screams of children
under the same sun.

How easily you could have been me.
How easily you could have loved a son
who would never allow you to look away.

I Only Remember Being a Bad Daughter

Mom blew up
the Minnie Mouse pool
on the third floor balcony
with desperate breaths.
I waited in my 2T one piece.

Why didn't she complain when
I dropped the pool toys off the edge
just to watch her run?
When I saw her beneath me,
grasping at mulch for wet plastic,
I scratched at an itch under my rib
where guilt was already blooming
and spreading like ground ivy.

And when I grasped the toy again in my pruny hands,
I didn't own enough words to tell her that
I knew I was bad. I knew I was bad.

Seeing JonBenet Ramsey's Photo for the First Time

My legs were swinging from a grocery cart.
Her face was level with mine from the tabloid stand.
She didn't look like me, my dark hair uncombed,
my wild, black eyes locked on her green ones: still,
cool, and beautiful. Fluorescent light
bounced from her glossy pout
to my blue raspberry-stained lips.

I saw myself reflected in her baby skin and felt
the intimacy that only young girls have:
if I offered her my lollipop, I knew she'd lick it and laugh.

I asked who she was. Mom tossed the milk
onto the conveyor and sighed,
A dead little girl.

That was the first time I realized I could die
without time or sick chipping at my bones.

To me, that's who she was:
a grocery store saint who died Christmas morning

to remind little girls like me
that you're not allowed to be
a little girl forever.

Bad Seed

They want me to be good so bad.

      For me to always be blooming.

I want that too, every morning

     when I pull my hair into two tight braids.

I think about pretty things I could own,

      and how I could own them.

The more I own, the more I am

       good and pretty.

But no one told me how.

       So I found out how to

pluck petals from others to add to my own

        bloom.

Safe and sheltered

        under mother's shade.

Even after she sees the

        naked stems quiver.

Because I will always be

        her flower.

Cyclic Vomiting Syndrome

Is it the Devil in me?
I feel her in my gut
at night, at the end of the month.
She cycles, like Mother
Nature but bile.

Am I going to throw up?
I need to ask my mother each night
before I slip and let sleep.
No, she needs to answer,
even if four hours later
she is changing my sheets.

No one knows but whatever Devil
is deep inside tugging at intestines
until I squeam, splash, shudder
with each sweet sick I lose
a little more of myself to clockwork.

Young Blood

Mr. Crone describes thick and thin blood.
My eyes roll back when I think
about what moves through me,
the map in me, whatever runs in those rivers.
Slow syrup or a bubbling waterfall
running from my heart.
When I fall, my head hits a desk,
leaves a gash. I dip my fingers
before heading to the nurse, show Mr. Crone.
Thin he answers.

II

What's using a tampon like?
Erin says it's like pulling your guts out by a string.
One tug and intestines fall into your palm,
bloody, brown, and pulsing
with your own life. Her long fingers curl
around the sweating Coke can and
I am afraid of those fingers,
the way she can pull

herself apart each month.
I am afraid of her fingers
finding the place where she starts.

Men Burned the Women. Girls Told Them To

A servant with no dowry, not a daughter,
Elizabeth
was diagnosed as under the affliction of an evil hand.

She threw fits, violent,
body hovering above her bed,
She screamed her throat raw,
beat knuckles bloody.

And once the night air met her lungs,
the reflection of the fire burned in her eyes,
and her body was still: she didn't recognize
the girl she had been.

Maybe she saw herself becoming them.
The women who burned.
Women who, thick-hipped, alone in shadows,
brewed cauldrons of steam.
For who?

Elizabeth knew
to burn or be burned,
and she chose to torch.

To the Dead Bat in the Parking Lot

I never knew you
were so small.
Wingspan tricked me,
nighttime sky blinded
while you flew away.

Bet you didn't know I was big.
I think about becoming smaller
most of the time.

You dropped dead on my Kia
and I whispered in your ear,
Do beautiful people
hold dead bats before school?
You said, *Please.*

Enfield Poltergeist

Janet Hodgson was 11 years old.
Marbles fell from her sky pelting her bones.
Chairs flew through her air bruising her skin.
Janet was afraid.
And no one believed. Until
Janet wasn't Janet anymore.

When Bill spoke through her, dry and dead,
men came. Not to help. To crouch in corners,
watching for, waiting for, wanting for
her to float, to speak, to scare.
Microphones followed her.
Cameras hid in her home.

Poltergeist prefer the province of a woman.
Pure, pubescent. And so did they.
After Bill said it was ok.

To Daughter a Devil

Every Girl conjures dead things
when she first bleeds.

Dead things don't smell the blood,
Girls can smell death now.

While Mommas mother with a sweet caress,
Girls daughter a Devil in their rooms at night.

It's not worth the wonder if it's something
in the gloss, something in the polish,

no Momma can say at what age Girls turn
from daughter to Devil.

Movies say good girls go bad
when someone slips in them
—spirits or bodies. Ask a Devil:
When are you done with daughters?

And a Devil flips through her date book,
slams it before saying,

Usually it's some summer in New York
when Mommas aren't Girls anymore.

Independence Day in the Wetlands

17 and you're still afraid of public bathrooms.
So, you part the marsh with bare feet, half a mile away
from lipstick-stained cups, you
slide cotton panties into mud and go.

You know it's not fair to leave panties
to be swallowed by green with the dying sky.
Still, you rub your big toe into the crotch, deeper,
pink floral gulped by something hungrier than you.

And that's when you learn that Earth is hungry
for whatever you have. And you haven't been
fighting her, you've been feeding her
with every buried body, every planted tree.

Until she spits them back, half digested,
too bitter for even her.
You finger the soggy cotton,
watch bright bombs in the salmon sky
and wonder whose daughter you are.

Your Reflection Kisses You Back with Tongue

Her cupid's bow dips deeper than yours.
You trace it when she stands
from her knees (where you pushed her).
There is no music in the mirror, she knows,
but you remind her every morning, naked,
tummy pouting like a fat bottom lip,
your thumbprints against the glass,
pushing dimples into her cheeks.
You kiss her to say, *I'm sorry.*
She kisses you to tell you that
she's tried talking to God,
but her mouth only moves with yours.

It's the House

who asks me to leave one morning.
She sighs and settles around me,
I peel my cheek from pillow, damp with drool.
What do I do, it asks, to make you pack?

I think that's mine, it says about the paperback I grab.
Her shutters quiver when I pass the vanity.
I've thought about cutting your hair while you sleep.
I put the hairbrush back.

The door doesn't creak when I walk out.
In the street, a parade of neighbors with sleep crusted eyes,
goosebumped in the dew. We all know, but still ask:
You too?

The Devil Shows You How to Use a Tampon

The first time you bleed,
the Devil comes to see.
She knows life can rent a room in you,
and that scares Mom, Dad, and
every boy you'll meet. But not her.

She sits on the edge of the tub, not there to convince,
but advise. And, as your fingernails grow redder,
she warns you, they blame blood for ghosts.
When you leave this bathroom,
the burden is on you.

And after she shows you how to
push, press, and pull inside yourself,
she grabs your daisy print panties from the ground,
throws them in the trash and tells you to
wash the last bit of sidewalk chalk from your hands.

If Gregor Samsa was a Girl

She woke with wings
never-feathered, but iridescent,
translucent, and quivering in dawn.

Her hunger was vibrating, vampiric. She craved
blood to drip through each Cheerio's belly
before sucking them through her spoon.

Her mother dropped her coffee
and screamed at her daughter
hovering in front of the fridge.

Shoo,   shoo,   shoo,
Shoo, shoo, shoo, shoo!
back to her room.

Later her brain would buzz with question marks
about the shape of growing up, growing down,
she needed to know

how to tell your own wings that you love them
shimmer-shaking as they percuss against your mother's skin,
your proboscis digging, swallowing.

Why She Declined Her Father's Invitation to Disney

The bucks in the basement
overhead, gazing empty eyed,
whispered that they were not always dead.
And they warned of Mickey Mouse
mounted next to them,
his smile drooping at the corners
after falling to his knees,
amid music and cotton–candied kids,
her father's rifle poised to shoot again.

My OCD Tells Me to Ask 'What Does It Feel Like to Be Beautiful' 5 Times before Looking in the Mirror

The first sin was a woman eating.
Brave isn't a bikini-wearing body,
it's a bite. A yellow, crooked bite
that fills your mouth with honey
and goes down like glass.
It's another bite, and another after that
until you are full of knowing
the lump in his throat
was caused by you.

Aphrodite Teaches Me

13-year-old girls need to bathe more than every other
Sunday night. She sits sudsy from sea on the edge of my bed.

But Mama—
Mama's a bitch

Mama won't let me. Wants to keep
the walls, tub, towels clean. Says I stink it up.

Crazy bitch.

She leads me to the bathroom.
Uses her pinky to pull off my nightgown,

her nail waking up a spine-long
trail of goosebumps.

Mama pounds on the door,
Aphrodite throws the shampoo bottle back,

her eyes on mine.
Always condition twice.

Four Girls Laying Under a Willow on June 10, 2020

They take their white cotton masks off,
and their honeysuckle breath blows
blonde strands that escaped from braids.
When girls group, they drape
themselves like satin, over each other.
Not to touch, to rest.
Quarantined together,
skin sticking, sweat living
in places razors missed.
Handing hairbrushes and lotion
back and forth and back again.
Limbs against limbs,
sleeping open-eyed outside.
Masks in the grass,
bare lips toward the clouds.

As long as trees last,
girls will be under them
shedding cloth and
asking the sun for more.

Taking a Nude Photo for a Boy Online

You never noticed your wings
until they start to shed feathers
with each big-eyed blink.
You strike a match and drop it in
the weightless white pile
for better light. The soft kind that shines on your
cheeks just right. When there's nothing left to burn,
you set yourself on fire.
Flames lick at skin,
your naked body framed by the blaze.
You press send, then stop, drop, roll,
Hot. Take it again,
but file down your horns.

Our Love is a Two-Headed Calf

After *Two-Headed Calf* by Laura Gilpin

In the morning we'll be carried, cold and limp,
survived by a poem like
a taxidermied calf on a shelf.
No, he didn't get to grow,
but he never flailed in pain,
never bleated for mercy.

Our love is that:
alive for a summer night
that tastes like sweet grass and rain.
And the stars have doubled for now
until we close our eyes,
the way young people do,
disbelieving in morning.

Monster

Dr. Hassan says I don't get a prize
after tapping each tooth.
Crushing ice with the pearly whites?
Close. Bones.
He jerks his hand out in time
for me to catch the tip
of his glove in my smile.

Bones can't lie.
They have little secrets, though.
They'll tell you they broke,
won't say how.
Blood won't tell you anything,
but it will tease.
And it stains your teeth.

Hungry?
Already ate, thanks.
I grin wet and red
to the dinner table.
Dad drops his fork,

and I explain
Dr. Hassan said this would happen.
cause I haven't been flossing.

My First Spell

Still 13 when I saw
someone had scraped the wisteria
from the mouse skull
I pocketed by the dumpster.
Peering through his eye sockets,
I knew I could grow life again.

I rubbed his snout round in algebra,
tucked it in my purlicue when I shook pompoms
toward home. The sunset singed
the hair on my neck before I could bite back.

Let's Get Fired Up,   Let's Get Fired Up,
We are Fired Up,   We are Fired Up.

When Brittany threw us —me and mouse—
in the clouds and we touched my toes,
the stands stood and saw

the spell between my legs,
the smell between my legs,

somewhere between my legs,
the solstice between my legs,

and wisteria bloomed again.

If Swan Lake Had a Happy Ending

Say Odette defeated Rothbart in the end.
Lived as a girl, married the prince, didn't jump.

Now when the prince touches her in the dark,
he comments on the quiver of her calf,
the flutter of her forearm.
She knows he means well.

But he has never been animal.
He has never missed a body
he was never meant to have.

The castle staff sees Odette sleepwalk,
trying to fly through the halls.
In the morning, they dress her
to hide the bruises,
the failures of her flight.

One night, they don't catch her.
And at midnight she wakes in water,
the lake where it started, wading and waiting
for feathers and beak to break skin,
for wings to grow from bone.

For body to become home.
But body never does.
Home never comes.

Horse Lashes

Samara, Samara,
you should be dead.

(Horses say that
when I want to sleep)

Samara, Samara,
brush your fucking hair.

I dream of horse lashes and legs
ripped off and out (Mama's too)

until the horses
stop talking.

Throw your wishes down this well.
Throw your daughter down this well.

A princess with pink cheeks
sings down this well.

Sings that someday someone
will come for her.

Maybe that's me
(it's always been me).

Seven days and the town will sigh.
Seven days and my hot breath comes back.

Dripping, crawling,
free.

If any God could have,
he would have

brushed my fucking
hair.

I Can't Talk to Ghosts, But They Can't Talk to Me Either

No tables rattle under my palms
when I ask for a name, a year,
for someone to grip and pull my ponytail
to red-scratch my back.
Movies say they want to bend my bones,

and whisper where they came from.
So I sleep with one foot uncovered,
begging the ghosts: touch, tug, take.
But they can't tell me that,

they don't have skin anymore, or toenails to paint pink.
They can't ask me the name
of the color peeking out from my sheets,
and I can't answer Flamingo Glow.

Madame Tussaud Makes a Death Mask of Marie Antionette in Madeleine Cemetery

She is an artist
and unafraid of how dead skin
feels against her thumbs,
like wax, like putty, something to mold.
She raises the severed head to her own,
studies it against the lamplight,
their faces share the glow
and she assures the queen,
I am doing this for you
So they will know you.
The head grows heavier,
aching to rest.

Blonde curls fall over her wrists, and she knows
it's just the wind flirting with the dead
when the queen's lashes quiver.
Still it's almost as if she is trying to blink.
Almost as if she is trying to whisper,
Gently, Madame,
gently.

Animal

I
It took one month after Mrs. Green died for Cali to nibble her
     nose.
She waited, perched on her chest.

Waited for her to scratch Cali's ear, to say her name
through a smile, deep and raspy, *Hungry, Cali?*

First it was one rough-tongued lick against her cheek.
Then a bite to wake her. Then blood

and more bites and more blood. And Cali was full,
sniffing at skin, she purred.

II
I called the police to check
on Mrs. Green after I hadn't seen her leave in weeks.

I guess animal control, the police said when asked what would
     happen
to the cat. Dogs get put down over this. Why not cats.

Cali didn't fight when I slipped her under my coat.

Just blinked when I let her go in her new home.

III
After licking her plate clean, Cali looks out the window
towards Mrs. Green's house, purring, pensive.

Then to me. Cali licks her lips as if to say
Someday.

10pm on 4th of July 2021

I walk the dog and watch the sky,
the artificial thunder rattles through his claws,
I imagine us walking into the fireworks,
the waterfall ones that start so high
you can barely see them before they rain down
like an American baptism of glitter and sulfur.
And I think of the British guy who got off
to the pictures I sent him before telling
me how fat and stupid Americans are.
I am fat and stupid.
I pretend that makes me brave.

A middle–aged couple stops to pet the dog.
The woman asks, Aren't you scared?
He is a small corgi but
nothing scares him,
not storms or fireworks,
Not him, I say.
She shakes her head.
I meant aren't you scared?
Alone, female in the dark.

The dog and I exchange looks
with the mutual understanding that
we are beasts in this world,
and we'll use our teeth when needed,
but it rarely is.

How I Became Bigfoot

I ask the man at a kiosk in the mall
how much it costs to forget what I look like,
and he hands me a map:
For you, $0.99.

It takes me an hour to get lost
and start breathing
the big-belly breaths
that children breathe
and I don't feel wild,
just less groomed.
I teach myself to ride a bike,
unafraid to fall.
I sing to the animals
and they sing back.
I sleep better than I ever have.

My husband, my 6th grade boyfriend, and the president
all think they see me out of the corner of their eye
and reach the silent conclusion: *No.*
She didn't know how to ride a bike.

I let myself wonder
if they've come up with some beautiful name
for the creature who floats
through the mossy trees. Until—
nailed to the dogwood,
feet from my bed of lilac,
a sketch of me and a call for
Bigfoot Dead or Alive.
I hold it like a mirror and wonder
if I can get my $0.99 back.

Eulogy for the Doe on the Side of State Route 128

I have passed her three times
—to home, to work, to home—
and each time I flinched
because I assume she was
a wife, a good wife.

In my rearview mirror, I see
her soap–soaked wedding ring twinkling
in fluorescent when she hugs her husband
after dishes are done, and
I see her kissing his antlers
in the doorway before work.

I see, on a bad night,
her husband ask if she'd stopped
taking her Prozac.
She didn't tell him
yes. Or that she was afraid
if she went to the doctor
for a refill that they would tell her
to lose weight.

The doctor's spittle would spray
as he told her it wasn't BDD or an ED
but her own body rotting
itself from the inside out.
Nothing she didn't know, but
hadn't heard out loud.

Instead she ran from him,
hooves hitting the road.
Her doe eyes closed
when the car came.
In that split second, she let herself imagine
a soul leaving her body
reborn as a human: hands on the wheel
blank stare on the road,
in a body hidden by a car, by clothes.

Or any body but a body
born with a target
—the bigger, the easier to shoot.

In an Effort to Stop Writing Poems About Dead Deer

I ask God to stop showing them to me,
but that's a big ask in rural Ohio where deer are brave, and I
    am not.
After prayer, before sleep,
He tells me what I've known:
Some people seek out lovers,
some people seek out God,
some seek out rotting doe
with eyes that look like their own.

Cicadas of Brood X

Last time they were here I was 8
and they covered the jungle gym.
On the swingset I let them bury me,
because we knew I was one of them,
ugly and loud.
With a red-eyed wink,
they flew away as quickly as they came,
wings pounding against their own body,
leaving me more naked than before.

17 years later, I see the first one again
and the pit in my stomach hardens,
and my pink peach flesh softens.
Will they comment on my body?
How it's grown its own topography
as they scale my hills and dip down my valleys,
their legs sinking deeper
when they land on my breast?

They do remember me.
Settling on my skin like they did,

they crawl through my curls, burrow in my braids,
and in a hiss that vibrates through my body, they say,
We love what you've done with your hair.

She Wasn't Afraid of Insects Anymore

When she walked through spiderwebs,
she didn't refuse the silk, she rubbed it
into her forearm like lotion.

When her shoe stuck in the mud,
she walked on, letting her foot meet Earth
again, again, again.

Her brain ached to lay down,
to live here, where webs and one bare foot
could disappear into some kind of decay
for Earth to play with until Earth was done.

But Earth wouldn't have her.
Grew their vines up and around her,
politely declining her skin.

She laid for two months before she knew
the birds were laughing at her wandering,
lazy eye, never quite focused on the sun.

So, she washed seeds down her tub.
Shone lights down the pipes,
watering with every shower,
and slowly they grew,

purple cornflowers who wanted
to crawl inside her, her mouth, her nose,
her bellybutton. They petal-whispered, *Open up.*

And she was buried, disappeared
under a field of flowers.
Hundreds of leaves, petals, stems,
and one blinking, lazy eye.

Superman Lands on My Balcony

gently, in a demi plie, after I've run outside

in my sports bra and boxer shorts screaming for his help.
Look, you've got to stop calling me like this.

I say, Superman, I'm about to do something bad.
I'm the villain here, someway,   somehow.

He ruffles my hair: I know the feeling, kid.
He flies away and I roll up the blue-prints

to my moon-destroying laser beam.
In my bed, I can see the moon peeking

through my blinds,
laughing at me,

and I pull my sheet up to my neck,
pinch it at my chin,

my flowered cape that will fly me, alone,
toward a sky blooming with explosion.

Dirty Doll

Tilly was 18 when her spirit jumped from her body
into the nearest pretty thing with ringlets and pink lips
where she thought she'd want to be forever.

Turns out she didn't want
to be anybody forever,
in any body forever.

And when Anna first set Tilly Doll on her dresser,
she admired her for an hour before kissing her soft cheek,
(now sticky and wet) and climbing into bed.

Every night Anna stared, kissed, slept,
and Tilly climbed to the highest shelf
and threw herself

to the ground, dreaming
of never being looked at again.

The Body Farm

Don't we deserve to know what happens underground?
To the bodies we've used, ran into the ground?
Bodies on bodies on bodies,
dropped, watched, studied on the Farm.

I don't mind knowing what will come of this body,
which insects will make me their home
(no better use for leftover bone).

But I am afraid, maybe selfishly,
that when I finally rest
someone will be watching me.

Carrie Moves to New York and Changes Her Last Name to Bradshaw

After she rose from the grave, she hopped on a train.
With cemetery dirt under her fingernails, she flipped through
      Vogue.

She got a perm. Her blonde hair bounced when she laughed
and she laughed more and more because

now she looked like the girls who tortured her.
Maybe now she was the girls who tortured her.

And in the mirror she saw for the first time what all that blood
had done for her skin.

And then she thought to herself that living and bleeding
and dying each month meant a little bit of pain and a whole
      lot of pleasure.

She wrote it down, to the girl in the shower
who was afraid of her body and the things it can do:

We bleed ourselves dry for seven days and live.
I have to wonder, why aren't we celebrating this?

After Finding Bed Bugs in Our First Apartment

We trap the first one in a baggie to set aside and inspect later.

We name him. The second one, too. We do this until
we run out of baggies and run out of names.

Before we break our lease,
leave bedless and poor,

we ask each other without words:
What if   we let them?

Some people don't react to bites.
We don't react to bites.

And didn't they live here before us?

We moved in and they smelled us,
crawled over our cuticles while we slept,

ate from our bodies without us waking.
And after they fed, hid deep in some spring.

But there is shame
to share your bed with hundreds of bodies,

to lose blood, unconscious,
with no scars the next morning,

to wash your own bloodstains from your sheets
and make your bed, again, for them.

I Ask My Realtor How to Keep the Ghosts the Same

I live in houses and meet ghosts who learn to live with me.
They don't ask why I'm here. I don't ask how they died.
We sit together the first week, watch *Dateline*. Each night
they count the breaths I take between sleep and wake.

In the morning I count the breaths beneath their sheet.
We lie, say the number is the same.
When I turn the key, when I leave
they stay. I move houses, the ghosts change.

In Pudica Pose

In season 9, episode 9 of *Seinfeld*,
Jerry dates a woman
who is comfortable with her own nudity.
He is not aroused for long
because, he says, there is a difference
between good naked and bad naked.
And he is disgusted with her body
squatting, coughing, living.

Even in the mirror I cover myself.
In pudica pose, recreating *The Birth of Venus*
to reach for my hairbrush.
When Venus touches her breast
and the space between her legs
there is shame.

Was Botticelli right?
Was Venus born
standing, modest, wistfully still?
Or was she born
squatting, coughing, hungry for life?

Snow White Takes a Nap After Cleaning the Bathroom That She Shares with 7 People

My wet hair clings to the tub,
black roadmaps of the places I could be
while I scrub the places I've been—
do I find the dirt, or does it find me?

I love these men, (or do)
I owe these men.

What is it like at the bottom of the well?
Is it clean? Every time I've jumped to see,
birds break my fall and carry me
to someone who says they need me.

I told my stepmother how tired I was
before she handed the me the apple
and told me to eat —that it would help me sleep.

Before I bit, I smiled,
Don't wake me.

Snow White Receives a DM from Dopey

And before she opens it
she knows what it says.
Or what she wants it to say.

The birds read over her shoulder,
the deer crane their necks through the open window to watch
her painted thumbs craft a response.

They remember the time years ago
when he walked in on her changing
and how he left, wordlessly and
how she has spent time with that memory
in every bed she's slept in since.

It starts innocently.
Now that she doesn't cook or clean,
Snow White has a lot of time on her hands to
read, watch movies, and write poetry,
and Dopey does well to feign interest
as she excitedly types to him and lets the birds braid her hair.

When she asks him, why now,
he admits to her after her bite, when she lay
motionless, speechless, gorgeous
she was the most beautiful thing he'd seen.
And looking at her Instagram photos,
posed, serene and silent reminded him.

For six months, every day while the prince is out,
Snow cradles her phone waiting for Dopey
to make her laugh, make her wet. He asks for pictures,
no clothes, eyes closed. Her animal friends help her pose.

Until one day when he tells her that he's moving in with his
            girlfriend.
Another dwarf who he pretends is Snow when they make love.
That means he doesn't need her anymore.
Dwarves don't leave princesses. But he does,
with a flowery message about two ships in some night.
He asks her not to write a poem about him.

And when Prince Charming comes home
to find Snow laying in bed surrounded
by dozens of apples chewed to the core,
mascara running down her cheeks,
he cradles and kisses her like he did that first time
and she remembers that he was the only one to try to wake

her.

The dwarves had kneeled, mourned and admired but didn't
       try.

Why didn't they try?

Snow White grabs the back of the prince's head
and kisses back for the first time.

How to Say I Love You to a Ghost

No one tells you there are five hours
between America and death.
You figure it out by asking him
to lick the first morning dew
from a blade of grass,
then counting on your fingers
to orient yourself
on your own American plane.

You talk in real time
and watch the same porn.
You can't touch him,
but you can feel
the smile under his sheet when
he tells you about the butterfly
—how her wing kissed his cheek.

Maybe the same one
that landed on your tongue,
after she teased you
without meaning to, by

loving and flying wherever
your heavy body stops you
from slipping in and out of.

So you indulged
the female desire
to rip things apart
with your teeth,
to crush monarchs
in your molars,
to eat and hate,
so you can love
in peace.

But if *I love you* is swallowed by
hours or caterpillars, know
when you see white sheets fluttering at dawn,
flirting with the newly blooming sun,
you'll remember,
Once, I ate butterflies,
I loved a ghost
and I was happy.

Some Summer

You wish you were autumn
—or just one autumn day—
as the wind tugs at your peach fuzz
when you step out of the makeup store
with $234 of makeup in your purse and
the $3 cotton balls bouncing
against your thigh in the plastic bag.
On the walk back to your car, it occurs to you
that when your mom told you
she was cheating on your dad,
she knew what it would do to you,
but she was too busy feeling the way you felt
when the one named Zack pushed into your dorm
and his tongue found yours before
you could pull the Crest Whitestrip from your teeth.
You still think you'll see him five years later
and impress him with your smile,
and he won't know if the shiver up his leg
is from you or the autumn day.

The horn of a car who wants your space
slaps you across the face and you know

you're some sticky, sweet summer
just like your mother.

Ghost Tour in Savannah, Georgia

Careless with her hearse
rattling over cobblestone,
the guide told us about innocent lives,
how their blood planted the seeds
of Spanish moss overhead.

Savannahians didn't hate us,
proud of their city and the bodies underneath.

A girl peddled a pink bike
in front of our hearse. Panic
from the girl's face
to tourists' who had paid
for this, for death.

We jerked,   lurched,   missed
pink bike, cherry toes.

An open palm to us,
and her flowered dress
caught fire in the setting sun.

She blazed blood orange bright,
made the hearse vibrate
between guilt and love.

Whose Hand Do You Hold When the Earth Ends?

When every nerve in your body glitters in anticipation of a
         blast
and every color you've ever seen dyes the sky at the same time?

Your mother's, your husband's,
the woman who handed you your fries at McDonald's?
At the end of the world or the end of the day, the hands are all
         the same.

CNN has a video to play in the event of the end of the world:
the Armed Forces marching band performing *Nearer my God
         to Thee*.
The same song the band on the Titanic played as they went
         down.

But let's say we won't be watching TV,
let's say we keep our hands to ourselves,
close our eyes and hope to see movies,

memories, bitter what-ifs behind our lids
instead of the black we've always seen.

So we go by ourselves in whatever ·
impact, implosion, explosion that ends us
eyes squeezed, still waiting for a poem.

After the Exorcism

When I come back to January
the fire is gone.

Before I dropped beads and bombs
until the bathwater turned pink,

until I couldn't see my own pink,
just the echo of drip,　　　　drip.

That was when the silhouette of horns
on the tile peered into me.

And I let him in.

Soon words weren't mine anymore.
Neither was my tongue, my lips,

my body. No one told me, but I understood:
I was free.

A circle of people around my bed who wanted to thaw me
from my own body, chip at my bones with their prayers.

If they knew I was warm, they wouldn't care.
I wasn't beautiful and they were scared.

Father, Father, fuck Father.
I am no one's daughter.

The last words it said, or the first words I said
back in my body, back in my mouth.

January doesn't have hot water anymore,
so I climb, clothed, in the tub.

Break the cobwebs with my heels and wait
for horns to make me ugly again, make me free.

After the Accident

I smell my blood before I see it.
Blood and gasoline swim
metallic and thick above my head,
tangling hair, warming my scalp.

Men rip the door from my car,
throw a sheet over my body for modesty,
I'm sorry I'm heavy.
The men I don't know laugh
and take me to the ambulance.

I'm breaking out in hives
and the doctor asks me if I want children.
Big red bumps bubble on my skin.
I watch them grow, my body a new planet,
red and rocky.
I may.

Nurses don't give me a chance to feel pain,
You didn't say you were allergic to morphine.
I've never eaten morphine before.
They groan, start a line of Dilaudid.

Children.
Your pelvis is shattered.
Odds are you won't be able to carry.
Carry? Children.

The rest of the day I fall in and out of sleep,
and I can't stop remembering
I was a baby once.

Acknowledgements

Thank you, Benjamin, for listening to every iteration of each and every one of these poems. Thank you, Mom and Dad, for supporting me since I first declared I wanted to be a writer.

Thank you to these outlets who gave these poems their first home:

"She Wasn't Afraid of Insects Anymore" first appeared in *Rogue Agent Journal*.

"Young Blood" was first published by *Drunk Monkeys*.

"It's the House" made its first appearance in *Mookychick*.

"After Rosemary Picked Up the Baby" first appeared in *Thimble Literary Magazine*.

"After the Exorcism" was originally published by *Peach Velvet Magazine*.

"After Finding Bed Bugs in Our First Apartment" first appeared in *Black Coffee Review*.

"I Asked My Realtor How to Keep the Ghosts the Same" first appeared in *Plainsongs Magazine*.

"If Gregor Samsa was a Girl" was first published in *Lammergeier* and was a *Best of the Net Nominee 2020*.

"After the Accident" first appeared in *The Raven Review*.

"Snow White Receives a DM From Dopey" was originally published in *Writer Shed Story*.

"How I Became Bigfoot" and "Eulogy for the Dead Doe on the Side of State Route 128" made their first appearance in *Contemporary Verse 2*.

About the Author

Megan Mary Moore holds an MFA in poetry from Miami University. She is the author of *Dwellers* (Unsolicited Press, 2019) and her work has appeared in *Rattle, Grist,* and *Contemporary Verse 2*. She lives in Cincinnati where she frequently dresses like a fairy princess, watches too many horror movies, and writes poems about things that scare her.

About Unsolicited Press

Unsolicited Press based out of Portland, Oregon and focuses on the works of the unsung and underrepresented. As a womxn-owned, all-volunteer small publisher that doesn't worry about profits as much as championing exceptional literature, we have the privilege of partnering with authors skirting the fringes of the lit world. We've worked with emerging and award-winning authors such as Shann Ray, Amy Shimshon-Santo, Brook Bhagat, Kris Amos, and John W. Bateman.

Learn more at unsolicitedpress.com. Find us on twitter and instagram.

CPSIA information can be obtained
at www.ICGtesting.com
Printed in the USA
BVHW030254250223
659219BV00007B/485